Nightmares and Ghost

Since a young age
I smelt the scent of sage.
Cleansing spirits
But one stayed and never went away.
I remember it like it was yesterday.
The games it played.
Notice things were rearranged.
When the light from the sky fades
As I lay.
In a corner He waits
Sinister and deranged.
In the shades
Engulfed by night.
When my dreams became
Days of pain.
Like my heart tried leaving
my rib cage.

Taking my breath then my pulse

Slowly fades.

Is there something wrong with my brain.

Am I insane?

I must be brave.

But it loves the hunt and chase.

To cut me with its blade

Back to it's cave, or make me

into a slave and put into a grave.

There is no escape.

Open me up eat until it's fulfilled.

Every night I watch it then.

Dreamed I got killed.

No one can hear my screams.

And my shrills.

I lost all my will.

It's harder to be.

Prescribed handful of pills

No one believes it's real.

So, I try my best to keep it in

I see it in my reflection.

Hail Mary for protection.

Walk Among Us

How much do really know about who is around?

How many not from this earth with an ultrasound

Try to see good remain hopeful now.

Inhabit bodies to get places they are not allowed.

How many killers in the crowd

The ones they didn't catch.

Would knowing help the mismatch.

What about the people praying on kids to snatch

Hotels involved now what the fuck is that.

It's getting crazy and blatant you better not lack.

What if someone died and came back

They just whipped another batch.

Like an egg that just hatched

So many homeless livings off trash

How long can they last?

Begging for small amounts of cash

Addicted to heroin and crack.

Feds investigations building up the facts.

Getting closer by being men of many hats

Thieves smash and grab running off like the flash.

Knives for protection but you would hate to get stabbed.

Then there's the luck one's never had a scratch

Stay away from the fads.

rocking Abercrombie and gap

Leaving petty problems in the past

Ignoring the complainers and the nags

You can be what you want transgender or just dressed in drag.

For whom you are or when you're from there's a represent flag

The everyday people that work for what they have

The ones barely hold their sadness together.

Breaking under pressure

Sickness and disability never getting better.

The youths that don't care whatsoever.

The few that find the end of the rainbow with hidden treasures

From business to the pleasures

Made through the endeavors.

It don't matter if any of them goes, there's always a successor.

Hoopty

I remember before I had I name.

Before I got those braids

When it was toys and videos games

I had this friend.

With a subscription to motor trend

I fell in love with cars.

Ferraris and Lamborghinis

And hot rods

To get one you had to be star.

Sitting on the steps

Watching them go pass trying see what they are.

It was mostly Toyotas and Honda Accords

They used to put them on the floor

Rims and custom bumping

A system that was thumping

the Beamer and the Benz

Had me really crushing.

Running and krumping

14 I started taking my mom's car like it was nothing.

the engine hummed

I remember how the dash lit up.

Seat back with my chin up

My niggas calling for a pickup.

Got my license a couple years later.

The first car was a geo prism.

Purple with cream interior

Cd folder in the front seat

Forget A to B

I was everywhere to Z

My Hoopty set me free.

But there wasn't a car I could keep.

They say you can tell a lot about man by way he treats his car.

I don't know what that's saying about me.

89 BMW, Ford Windstar, Dodge Neon
Altima's and Maximas, Honda Civic Acura and infinity's

Back then a Hoopty was perfectly affordable.

Just a little rickety

But it kept me on my gitgetty

Not giving a flying fliggetty

But this jammed door is messing up.

My chivalry

And no heat made me shivery.

If someone hit me, I'm faking an injury.

Pray it starts hope that stops.

But I'm ride this Hoopty

until the wheels fall off

Love language

Your kind heart.

Makes mind spark.

Wanting to know how to feel.

Because your vibe is real

A nice sense of humor

Speaks volumes to who you are.

Medicated laughter

You do your thing in the kitchen not a bite I would pass up.

Your flow is the reason you glow.

Black and beautiful

Not a single part is cracked up.

Your style could make,

a glass eye shatter

Allways there when it really matters.

Speaking positive affirmations

Understand good things come with patients.

If circumstances had us separated
I know you would be there waiting.
To be my safe haven
Your home nowhere near basic
Real art and exotic flowers in
Compliments to the mother lands
Gifted you shape.
Our kids are in the yard playing behind the gate.
Gracious soft spoken,
listening and understanding is your greatness.
I hold doors but you hold places.
They say when a man finds a woman.
He found a good thing.
Nothing could compare except
A halo and some wings
Not only praying for us to win
But for
Hunger and wars to end
Never afraid to give.

Always seeking perfection

Not comfortable when stress needs addressing.

Honesty is reserved for the best of friendships.

Your Gods most impressive invention

With that Hennessy

(Say with that Hennessy after every line)

I can't feel.

You can put my life on a reel.

It created a shield.

Front lining in the field

Walking with it unconcealed

My pain stays healed.

I just want to be happy.

I'm a walk down an alley.

There's no gravity.

Dress real flashy

Sell all my baggies.

Holler at every woman with a fatty

If I have three some

give both a wedding ring.

I can do anything.

Celebrate life confetti and silly string.

30 pieces buffalo chicken wings.

Fuck with my family I'm jumping in.

I don't care what people think of me.

No more stress

Say it with your chest.

Liquor on my breath

I blew my whole check.

Go and see my ex.

Putting hickies on your neck

Sing along to every song.

Getting all the words wrong

Drink it until it's gone.

I'm a fuck her raw

From the whole in draws

Take the keys to my car.

I'm a spend the night.

I might steal your sons bike

Get into fight.

I could lose my life.

Double eyesight

Can't see the time on the clock.

You gonna have to help me walk.

Daylight got me in shocked.

Don't remember that we talked.

Fall in a coma.

Good thing my drinking days are over.

Slap on the Wrist

I'm not sure when I stopped giving a fuck.

Probably the same time I realized nothing was ever enough.

Lies, secrets and broken laws could determine trust.

Especially when all we have is us.

I lost count how many times I been in cuffs.

Couldn't be seen with all that church.

Breaking and entering for all it's worth

Surrounded the crib with k9s and guns drawn.

surrender on the front lawn

Dead wrong

I was going where I belong.

Stole couple cars.

Learning shoptalk

Got pulled over.

Didn't make it far.

Assault and battery with a dangerous weapon

All because I stomped someone out.

Fallout every school kicked me out.

You would think I learned lesson.

in time weed was a class B drug possession

Pulled the rug lost the plug.

I was the perception.

Of the cultural misconceptions

This is not a confession.

It's all public records.

littering at the train station for not putting a can in the trash

disturbing the peace responsible for the music to loud and an unruly crowd

Pulled over more than 30 times, no license, no registration, attached plates and no insurance.

Probation fines paid

What a waste

time

I atoned for some my sinning.

Couple cases was dismissed.

Continuing without a finding

Years of trying to keep control.

Not before a Court date every couple month

Might as well plead guilty.

No reason to run.

It's just a slap on the wrist.

Fingerprint

Take my mug shot.

I don't have to say shit.

Except I don't want no sandwich

Take everything I own.

Put me in the hold.

Carve my name in bold.

Pay my bail let me go.

Concept Elevation

A darker skin

I am chosen.

With big inner beast

There's real in me.

That won't sacrifice in defeat.

Why would I settle for less

can't be weak.

Always in a state of elevation

In control of my direction like a air station

Power the rocket we headed to space into constellations.

Tell yourself you are amazing.

Tell yourself do it now.

No time is not waiting.

Develop your skills in preparation.

Make it 2 Made it

Cause you can't make it unless you made it

Speak clear and loud communication.

Whispering no secrets

small goals are still achieving.

Failure is just a visitation,

remove the negative like a amputation.

Flexible bend without breaking.

Seek knowledge and translation.

Hustle in every language

Let your ambition become stimulation

Let the animal awaken

Destroying anything that comes in the way like a fixation.

Until it's ashes and dust bottles it up like a cremation

Do away with lazy affiliation,

holding you down

I will become greatness

No matter how many times you have to say it

It has to voice the narration

Winning is running through your circulation

Thickening it's concentration

I will, I can, the motivation

A million times like a incantation

Creating good vibrations

Energy 2 True believe in the transformation

A higher being A Godly incarnation

I better version all ways improving to liberation.

Free to what you want when you want

without stipulation.

Queens

I love y'all from my grandma mama auntie cousin's sister's niece's wife and my daughters

I'm proud to be in your lives as a son brother nephew uncle husband and father.

It's very important you know y'all played a big role in the man I am today it made me a lot stronger.

I may not understand everything y'all go through, but I would die before dishonor.

Caring nurturing understanding nonjudgmental beautiful smart funny passionate innocent and loyal.

You are all royal

Worthy of the world it would be perfect with your control the contribution can't go unseen.

giving more life than soil

You can do anything but blow us out of the waters.

When it comes to teaching, doctors, nurses,

Writers,' singers. dancers parenting, judges, scientist and problem solvers

The list goes on best of all using words against your rivals.

We may see ourselves like the rocks of Gibraltar Hercules

But you are the guns and bullets underneath gates to the sea ready to go to war with me a

warriorist

Thanks to you we exist.

Your Presents are always missed.

We are unable without your assist.

Checking every box in what is needed in life's list.

Kings

We are our brother's keeper,

But I'm most cases,

We are our brothers maker.

Not seeing the influences

And how it's shapes us.

But there so many good things in

Our nature

I don't understand why the world becomes our breaker.

So many continue to hate us.

No matter how much we try nothing goes in our favor.

To be honest some of us mess up now and later

But could be understood if you peel back the layers.

How would you feel if you would do anything for your family,

And they still forsake us.

Targeted for our complexion and rarely heard inside a prayer.

Used for a green piece of paper.

Abandoned by men with no intention to raise us.

Only when we are successful people tend to claim us.

But staying in our place don't speak up share our belief is the full disclaimer.

Always on the topic of who's real or who's faker.

We must give up our lives in life-or-death situations but do anything to contain us.

Over sentencing and enslave us

Chase beat shoot and use tasers

Even though they know what could happen to us those calls are coming from our neighbors.

Work hard do most of the back breaking labor.

We must be big and strong for you to feel safer and at the same time in danger.

Get married just become a player.

When it's over a legal caper

What's hers is hers even what's yours

Can't even afford to cure your bellyachers.

And everyone still coming for petty favors.

In return there's nothing they can trade for

Say no and get treated like a traitor.

Can't be short can't be fat have a car a job can't be bald is the way they grade us

The world wants everything delivered hand and foot like we the waiters.

There's nowhere we can yell or express our angers.

It's like asthma with no inhaler.

They won't even let us breathe I guess only the lord can be our witness and vindicator.

The written order for Great fathers' providers husbands' sons' protectors

Noble with honor respectful responsible intelligent loving and caring with good principles and morals.

Never give up, That is our allocator

Us or the U.S

The irony of what money is made of you wouldn't believe 75 % cotton.

It's so difficult to understand how we are in debt and have so many problems.

We print money in Washington or Texas you would think we are running out of pollens.

Government constantly talking about shutting down.

When they are unhappy with their amount

Inflation got us so we can't afford anything now.

Why hasn't minimum wage increased with the cost of living?

The president always wants to announce the economy is on the rebound.

But homelessness is forming crowds.

Immigrants crossing borders and every one of them housed.

So many drugs and addiction

Senseless crimes endless victims

You wouldn't believe the hate and separation without a cellphone witness.

Everyone is starting a business.

Food is not food it's causing so much illness.

Waters are unsafe for drinking.

How was Covid a sickness the created so much richness?

We were told we needed Hurd immunity.

So, to get vaccinated we give in

But we didn't ever get it.

It killed anyone regardless of their fitness.

Something just seems suspicious.

We are sending Ukrainians millions.

Brick unity will create A financial division.

A currency backed by gold.

More powerful than the dollars and the euros

New larger interest rates for cars and homes

Being drove out communities we fought for raising rental prices forcing us to go.

The banks use our money to give out loans and we can't even get our own.

The U.S has been exposed.

They're using us keeping us under their control.

Building the strength, of our bones

And the heart of our souls

With all the lies told

Peace Young King

First off where y'all getting these guns from

Whoever put it in your hand money or not your bro or your brother or any other person claiming to love ya

They know you will lose your life, grave or the cell.

That's the true meaning of a mother fucker.

Young as y'all are there shouldn't be a reason to take it that far to pick one up.

Once it's done, your life will never be the same.

We done gone through it, sometimes you can't walk away.

what it does is

They see as weak try you every day of week.

Don't like the way you are getting rubbed.

Bumped and nudged.

They start acting dumb.

And no one is going to run.

Involved in gangs either streets against streets and crips or the bloods.

You can choose not to be a thug

There plenty of citizens that stay out that life living good in our hoods

I really don't want this to sound like telling anyone what to do

Everything has consequences take a minute before you choose

What is a win

What is a lose

Find a counselor and a therapist.

Every move must be intelligent.

A lot of fathers are gone find an adult you trust to delegate before it takes you out your element

Y'all young kings please tell if your life is in danger

There are people that help with licenses for their weapons.

And a legal system that can fight for you with evidence.

Not Snitching is for people in streets.

So, go get the help that you need

Please

There's Kings your age that will never be freed

Mothers that cried begged and plead

Can't believe you can't even breathe

Hold your breath and close your eyes, that moment when can't hold try a little bit longer

That's what dying feels like challenge

To stop the violence

Someone needs to start the conversation

These kings are fighting in private

A nonprofit for those suffering in silence

To operate without bias

Private Beach

I finally found some peace
A nice quiet beach
It's given my life a new lease
At first it was place to think of the deceased
And try to release
Took me a while just to get out of the Jeep
With roses on the seat
Walk across the sand and drop it in the sea
I would go a couple times a week
And stare in disbelief
The air helping me breathe
Is just my coping technique
Every moment is unique
Lay in the grass close by until I fall asleep
My melanin increased

Visibly unconfined

A place from heaven, carefully designed.

Slowing down the time

Helping me unwind

Embracing the unshaded shine

My mind realigned

Realized I must survive.

I smiled I cried, but I have to set my feelings aside.

Walk and talk with pride

Let love and happiness combine

Remind to live, laugh and always be kind

Find my inner child

With eyes so wide

Optimistic with nothing to hide

Not a cloud in the sky

Disregard the how could this be or why

got down to meditation and focus

on making my life better I have to try

Try

See to the occasion and rise.

Watch and follow signs

I soar and fly.

Try

Try never living a lie.

Until I'm that guy

Try

She said

Stay busy be strong

And you'll be fine.

Want to be Wanted

Without pardon

I want to be wanted.

No excuses the desire of your privilege

Bonnie and Clyde

This love is deadly and vintage.

Me the first of your three wishes

A well thought out decision.

Lips tremble thinking of kisses

Want to be wanted.

Can't be outsmart, exactly what's wanted

Dreaming of that pussy till my thoughts are rotten.

Pounded and rodded

I get you jolted and started.

Endless spark to our connection

Your only selection

Apart is like a demise that haunts her.

A missed call and she will need a sponsor

Might collect my personal items and conjure.

Together we're stronger

There's no war we can't conquer

Engaging in horrors

If anyone harms her

10 times the trauma

Do the same for me, I'm your partner.

Passion beyond this world

Find each other in other lifetimes.

I am yours

Our souls reserved.

Stirred and merged

Every ingredient the makings of you

There's no diluting this stew

There's no me without you.

The beginning of our justice

Just us

and nothing but the truth

Like the stand in a court room

Wish for you

This more than a gift

With wrapping paper and a box

It's meant to uplift.

When you're feeling low

You don't have to show.

What we already know

Life's been moving slow.

God bless you with wealth and health.

And what you been waiting for excels

Accomplishments hang over yourself.

Like a champions belt

Where there is one there shall be many

The lord is cooking so good you can taste the smell.

A spell prepared after Twelve

The darkest hour in another realm

Go ahead celebrate every day

I hope you get the upper hand with all the cards you are delt.

No one can fuck with you.

Camouflage and stealth

May you be hidden well

From all the lies the devil tells

And your name rings bells

Keep your family strong and together.

Love live long without measure

smile always shine bright.

Your theme song sounds of treasure

Never wrongs where you call shelter

Acres for a yard the sun smoothen your texture.

Everyday you're looking better

Children are successful to the point of a new level.

Goals arrive ahead of schedule

Five generations each one done something special

A love that end with matching grave sites

Husband and wife

To be continued in the afterlife in paradise

Fuck this job

(Say fuck this job before every line)

I'm about to move work like sully Dushane,
And them men dem in the yard

I don't care how many times they call
Make up some shit like my car just stalled
I'm thinking about faking a fall
Hit the snooze button 10 times on my alarm
Nobody better not say shit today
If you're looking for help the answer is go way
I'm calling out on pay day
Ordering the shrimp and the steak
I need a raise

Find someone else I'm not staying late

I'll be the last one back from my break

Looking for me like Patrice Rushen

No, I can't pick up the pace

The first one out the gate

Go ahead speak to my manager

Next Karen I see I'm a strangle her

Throw these boxes don't care if I damaged them

I don't even smoke but when they go outside, they my friends

Hide in the bathroom pretend, like my phone was ringing again

I'm so close to stealing out this register

Why you putting it on a pedestal

Took all this tax for, state and the federal

Take me off the schedule

I know someone this is better fa

Fuck the policy me and lady from accounting been sexual

I ate your sandwich

Im going to sleep

Play the lottery every night pray I become a millionaire

I ain't never cared

Haitian

You don't get to choose where you come from

I wouldn't have it any other way, what's done is done.

You should know My parents are Haitian I was raised in the city, so I am not the one.

How it began is a story known by everyone

Slaves from Africa fought for their freedom and won.

And built the eighth wonder of the world

Surrounded by mountains and ocean

But also supported and helped free Venezuela, Bolivia, Colombia, Ecuador, Peru, and Panama

Fought in the battle of Savanna

As the free men of color

Against the British in Georgia

We are revolutionary warriors

So you have to understand why

Even after people have so much negative things to say

we have pride

We wouldn't dare shame the many that died

The food to me is Devine

No matter the recipe you find

Griyo ,bun-nun, suos pwa, legume,

Diri Colai and jon jon , soup joumu, taso,

It hurt when I heard in the earthquake, a quarter of a million lost their lives.

I always wanted to go and see it how,

My elders described

I may have lost the opportunity.

But always found unity in my community

I have to stay true to me

The language spoken with intensity so beautifully

I hung on Every word on the radio how we couldn't live suitably

The mutiny divided the island the president
was murdered brutally

Civilians be chased out their home

Leaving everything behind the only avoid

Being killed or things being destroyed

Finding a way to America

We will make a way, we always have.

We are going get employed

We will go to church and spread all of or joy

If one thing is for sure

Strength will be restored

I love you Haiti, holla at your boy.

Alone with Music

Just me my music

Breaking our bond is useless

A good mood trip

My bodies coolant

Teaching your mind what the truth is

It is it, that's choosing.

Realizing that the shoe fits

Blood sweat and tears the soundtrack to my group pic.

Before I get suited

letting the videos be my blueprint

Following the flows of lyrical word smiths

Inescapable like twin Uzi's shooting

Motivating my movements

The drums and melody got me bopping my head.

Echoing my minds amusement

Becoming part translucent a mutant

Getting rid of the fog and pollution

In a space of my own pursuant

Just me and my music

Maybe adding piff and drank undiluted.

Late summer night cruises

Proven to loosen.

Tension or even be Cupid

always Playing, even showering and grooming

But it can get gully like the unit.

Showmanship of a student

But a dropout

Study it like a course, the lox invade my thoughts and move in

Believe it or not music is my institution

Dim lighting illuming

But my imagination is blooming

Exciting every nerve blowing all the fuses

Adopting its cultural methods like a recruitment

Kill the vibe and get booted.

You don't have to understand it but you will respect the achievement

From the mud and pavement

To 6 figure payments just for what you saying

Just me my music proven,

To be at your truest and lucid

Grooving since the wombling

Paper in my cassette making mixes like I know what I'm doing

The dj with my favorite songs on replay thinking outside the cubic

If you interrupt me, I might lose it.

Respect my time when I'm alone with music.

Never forget what you did for me

First, I would like to thank god

I know looking out for me is a full-time job through good and bad, you were there for it all

I am not going to lie at my worst you even answering the call.

With no one to turn to you were able to keep me calm.

It had to be like defusing a bomb.

Grateful to wake up every day happy enough to put on my god given charm.

Secondly another reason why I'm here and I know any gospel songs is because of my mom.

I don't think I will ever witness another person working so hard.

Her example of good at a genuine level will last so long.

Is the realest reason to love, I am so drawn

I can see past flaws

That left deep and noticeable scars

You taught so much about life and the importance of family.

And can be shown by what you do carefully.

And how to fight during tragedy

Do without expectations happily.

I have to shout out my brothers and all the knowledge that they have for me.

It's like someone testing everything before you then letting you know if it's ok.

They wouldn't harm me in known way

Took guns out of my hand I don't see how I can repay

To my aunt that opened her doors to me when I had no place

And never made me feel like I over welcomed my stay

My friends accepted me and let me go at my own pace.

So, our relationships are still in great shape

Walked to a place even if could of sealed our fate.

Riders

Fist bump then hit my chest plate.

So many memories I wouldn't trade

Especially my wife we been down since a young age.

10th grade

Experience every faze.

For you I pray

Too deep to ever end this love is 19 years prepaid.

I love all the time I spent with my children worth trillions.

Treat it like team building

Do without blinking

Can't forget my favorite store it's crazy how loyalty turns into trust.

Some days that walk, met by good energy it was like they love to see you winning.

It was more than just business.

One of the very few trying to help me and still is.

Watt up Lu

There would be worse days without you.

To everyone else that stopped when our paths have crossed, I won't forget what you done for me and that's the truth

I'm Back

I'm back now say less
Used to wear Caterpillars from Payless
Hotter than summer
Dark as the winter solstice
Fiery night
I'm trying to be nice.
Paid the price.
Hustle till I can't no more
Then do it some more.
My feet are getting sore like a soldier.
But there's custom Italian Sandals
At the door
Like I got 100 fiends
My wolves find you.
Like you are pissing on trees

Damn black

How many bullets you think you need

I had problems that would make you

Ask for help Spiritually.

Please don't be finished with me

Try take advantage of my susceptibilities.

With a addiction to nicotine

A death you don't get for free.

Distracted by the women I see

Satisfied another freak

Give her the rock Johnson like my name is Dwayne.

You know my clout

We don't have to speak

First let's roll and get geeked

Forget the haters and doubts

Curl the toes on your feet

Pressing you like I'm in a arcade

My mattress a cloud so,

No complaining this week

She likes to be restrained

Gagged so she can't shout

Buy some new sheets

Felling my pain

I'm well endowed

smoking blunts at the beach

Most don't make it out the crime that created fame.

schooling putting on about

How …. not for the weak

It's a dirty game

Only the strong can account

Listen when I speak

Do them all the same

Never trust, if your men didn't vouch

Black Canvas

The world is vast, but it changes fast, small minds ignore the past.

I see the perfect colors of contrast dedicated in my meditating.

They meshed and twirled but is, a

unshaken creation

The blackest canvas with an orange bolts

Red skies green clouds

The sun is grey.

The moon is brown

Gold trees and platinum grounds

Volcanic white lava

Bubbling under purple water

Rain is teal that flows upward

With hurricane funnels

Lavender Mountains crumble

Peach snow all the way to its tunnel

Fungal huddled around a drummer

Next to a bed of ivory bones

with lovers

Their brown skin cuddle,

As they hover

Your Gonna Live

Despite the diagnosis
The lord has spoken.
Follow him like Moses,
To the faithful he owes us
Even when it seems hopeless,
That's when God is the closest
Look at the glory he has shown us.
Please remain focused.
The only one who really knows us,
The love is your bonus.
Speaking to the voiceless
Even with wrong choices
Took the wheel yes, he drove us
Except the blood and the body
It is potent.
You don't have to wait in the lobby,

The gates are open

Blessings without notice

This is your moment.

Defeating every opponent

You can see your power is growing.

Worship say his name Jesus

And provoke him

In the name of the Holy Spirit and son

Your gonna live.

The air to your lungs

Don't worry about a lifetime,

When eternity is a beautiful one

You're no longer racing.

now you don't have to run.

Rejoice his heart has sung.

Listen to the thump

Look what your life has become

You are second to none

Taken the weight even in tons

His will can never be undone

There's no equivalent sum
Past the sun and the love
From the heavens above
Let go all grieving and grudge
Your gonna live
In gods' arms can you feel his hug
Your illness has vanished
Your soul replenished
The key to getting through
Your darkest days is the pianist
The one to stand with
With the keys to planning
You know he would laugh if man did

Know what I'm talking about

(Say know what I'm talking about, After every line)

Behind the store stash the hammer

Your paper based on how long, you can stand up

Poo shiesty and a hoodie we don't give a fuck about a camera

You hyped me now she a groupie got a reputation for stamina

If I catch a case and get away I'm find a place and I ain't coming out

Threatening the jury and sticking to the story all I need is reasonable doubt

in a suburban music blasting no more rules on the sabbath tied up in the trunk for running your mouth

We don't praise the sun of the morning so you catch me under the moon star light

Durags and waves a classic man lighting cigars with a match stick in control like a doom bar bike

The room can get real dysfunctional glass breaking you don't know where the shots are coming from so who you gon fight

I'm a get a bottle for us to drink when we link more magical than shrooms on prom night

I done came from the gutta but I want better so my kids are doing all right

I nigga always wanna chill when he got no life watching it flash before you like a strobe light

I do it for family I love hard keep them close to me we don't have any enemies

You can count on me before you get to three sooner than eventually there's more to dedication than the eyes can see

all I need is your honesty weather I'm right or
I'm wrong too much with the trickery and
worthless bribery

A wolf in crowd of sheep silently sharpened
my teeth on the cowardly in fiery climate
streets

Outer Body Conciseness

There is a leak somewhere

Voices floating around midair.

Unattached but connected and very aware,

Far enough to frighten and still feel near.

The worst part it doesn't even care

An announcement demanding what it declared.

Trying to reasonably denounce its ability making us a twisted pair

Good or bad just knowing it's existents.

Shouldn't be here

Captivating your attention like a emergency flare

A virus in the software

Ideas you wouldn't share

But the drive is clear

Gotta get paid in full, I got stack 4 Ace like I'm playing solitaire

Get husky then fall back like a grizzly bear.

Ambitious to free enough to do nothing neckwear covering my chest hair.

Analyze every scenario just to get there

Operating out of fear

Just the thought of struggling I get scared.

Isolation before venturing out to prepare.

Like checking my own squares

In my questionnaire

Are you ready?

Keep going, no breaks no landing gear

Jumping to conclusions an illusion a world engineered

Are the motives insincere?

Is My Consciousness the puppeteer.

Or is there an outside entity I hear

Which direction do I steer?

Looking for a related lead volunteer

My paranoia hung over me like crawling under meat hooks.

Start see deadly visions and I'm the star of the premiere.

Could I ever be fully excepted with this Sabotaged character Smear?

Scheming I should have Cauliflower ear,

These voices are damaging.

My only wish is to go back to normalcy forever I swear

Davon great Pride

Your mother and I were inseparable.

You were a surprise to us at 16 but really it was Inevitable.

We didn't even really talk much about what to do.

turns out the experience was incredible,

You made everyone so happy before you were even delivered.

It was magical like it was made real by a wizard.

Every weekend, movie and dinner

Your mother's skin glowed and her eyes shimmered

I got to cut the umbilical cord

My mother and your mother's grandmother held you like an award.

First thing the doctors said would look at the balls on that boy.

Which is crazy as you grew there was so much fear you ignored.

You always wanted to know more

You always wanted to be around adults.

I never seen you bored.

I remember the first time you seen seeds after an apple was cut, you said dad did it pop pu itself

My hope for this world was restored.

You were adored

It's crazy through the years you were good at every sport.

Did your homework and your chores.

Didn't get into drinking doing drugs or skipping still have a clean record.

Thoughtful and kind a real gentleman

Wasn't running around chasing women

Everything you started you finished.

Especially the big plates of dinner

you

never was a quitter

Just did it

Never asked for much and didn't fuss if we couldn't get it

I'm proud of the man you're becoming.

The person you are

ahead of a new generation next to them, it's circles your running

Janiyah's Beautiful Heart

I don't know if I should say this but honestly you almost weren't here

We were torn over the decision when a protester help us see clear.

It was the best thing I ever did with my life and it's scary to think of

I never knew someone could create so much love.

We didn't want to know your gender so when the midwife yelled it's a girl.

I Immediately started thinking of this world.

Worked nights and did what I could during the day, you had to be safe cared for, of that I was sure.

The cutest chocolate bald baby when you laughed my worries was cured.

You were apprehensive making friends but that only made us closer more.

It took so long to let you go even though it was like your feet wouldn't grow and you walked slow.

I remember the summer you learned to fly a kite and ride a bike.

Your personality started to show.

You could keep up with the boys.

So much tougher than them and didn't let anyone push you around.

But behind it you were sensitive to it all

Just seeing people hurt cry or emotional song had you in tears from your frown down to the ground.

It seemed like a kitten was the support you needed now.

Caring for it like a baby.

Emotion you could give without disappointment.

From a pet

Somehow it relieves your stress.

You held a lot of pain in and really did your best.

But that's only because you lost so much

You were losing faith and trust.

I'm glad you were able to build your confidence back up

And like star with gold dust you found a way to adjust

You realized you are enough.

Anyone should be fortunate to have a place in your heart.

And family has the biggest part.

AJ Prince of Swagger

Timberland sweatsuit for your baby picture

Your first expression was the middle finger.

Everyone thought you were handsome, the perfect mixture.

I have never seen so many visitors.

It was like people wanted to live with us.

You were crawling so young we had to put you in a baby walker.

You ran before you walked nothing could stop ya

You were our Buddha baby but your energy was like Biggie, so your mama called you Papa

Even when you took pictures we knew you going to be a problem.

You were the kid everyone talked of

How you were so smart, was what they were so shocked of

And I guess that's why you always had a dollar.

You are what you get, when a prayer is answered.

As you got older you rarely got mad, always cool tempered, never had any tantrums.

Polite a lover not a fighter

It was like you could sense what really matters.

You had confidence and seemed responsible, that was your swagger.

But you did have a humble chapter.

The first time you were less than happy was during Covid.

After you worked on yourself the transformation couldn't go unnoticed

But you proved even when things are hopeless you can fix whatever is broken.

You don't know this, people started naming the kids after you like a prince you were already know where you're going

Amira's sense of humor

Your mother and I had an incomparable compatibility.

We were from the same hood and went through similar adversities.

Had to look out for a younger sibling when our sick mothers couldn't.

Our connection was extremely explosive and loving at the same time.

You were conceived in celebration of love, our baby valentine.

You cried nonstop when it was just us two without your mother.

I was so scared that you didn't like me

And you looked more like me than any of my others.

I knew no matter how long it took my parenting would be rediscovered.

Then everyone got dressed up for you to be baptized at a small church

And out the blue in the lord's house

Our father and daughter relationship was forged.

I was so happy I knew things would be different when we walked out those doors.

All you wanted to do was play it was like I was your favorite toy.

Knocking my hat off my head and pulling on my beard you thought it was so funny when I pretended to get upset.

Running all over the park we had to do the obstacles together,

Your laughter I will never forget.

I can't remember anymore, you ever being upset.

We went to Chucky Cheese and stayed for hours not a minute I would regret.

even though I didn't have any energy left.

On your birthdays I seen you were a little shy like me with too many people around

So, I was a uniformed clown

Only when your favorite show was on you wasn't jumping up and down.

We talked so much I'm glad to be an ear you can loan

You had a thing for making funny noises and farting sounds.

No matter how many times you laughed it seemed to never get old.

I admire the sense of humor you owned.

To match your smile not even to the tooth fairy it could be sold.

Max Payne

I be gripping pistols two at a time.

double tap

It will be quick when you die.

Fuck two phones give a 45 and 9

They be running, like where the fuck you gonna hide.

She said she love thugs, like ok what the fuck is your sign.

Do a tune up and an inspection before I put the bricks in the ride.

Switch plates add bumpers stickers you know I'm a shine.

Better get a money machine, Boy I'm moving with pride

No middleman what I make is mine

If see me on my grind say watt up but tomorrow, you better act like you blind

Dope cologne and fresh breath

Getting old watching every step

fuck her good after a haircut.

And I just cashed a check

It's getting hot we are popping off.

Just a reminder I got 2 Glocks,

Laura Croft

Let my son hold my cross

And pray to God he doesn't get stopped

Don't punish us for who we are

Never talk it's still and always been,

Fuck the cops.

How you scared of your job

If the Rico is a charge

Then your organization is the cause

I don't fly no planes or drive no boats,

There's no terrain for it to grow,

Are you insane? Is this a joke?

I know it's not you all,

But it's a shame what known and

Let it go.

We are the only ones you control.

The hustle gives us hope.

Where we are slain another has rose

Where there's rain the road will overflow

The sky opens.

Usually before it does the most.

The eyes die.

You're staring at ghosts.

I'm just trying to pick the wreck on the road.

At Home

Tossing and turning is part of my sleep pattern.

Travel many moons in my own space like Saturn.

A Big Bang surrounded me with all that matters.

Pieces of my peace built with a large ax and hammer.

The king of my world uphold only to my living standards.

Undiscovered to many not even with Hieroglyphs and a lanterns

The power isn't shut down, but every corner is lit with candles.

Scented with fresh linens and summer breeze tangle.

Phone ringing but I'm not concerned with the rumors and shambles.

TV set to the music channel

Head sunken into my pillow heavier than an anvil

Feet up cushion underneath my ankles

rent at times may seem more than what I can handle.

It's still emptying my mind to make it tranquil.

Even though it's Feng shui it's only going one way with my AK on the mantle.

Draws off black navy-blue flannel panel short on let my balls dangle like a triangle.

Pop up without calling and get your welcome canceled.

But the ones in the smoke with me I'm so thankful.

So many memories I don't want to see outside might as well put me in shackles.

My home is the beach, and my phone could be fucking with granules.

Distracted by internet models.

Making your relationship hostel

Keep the wifey happy or watch the kingdom get toppled.

My number one rule is not to be verbally harmful, real men don't argue,

And keep your business handled.

For It

Believe what you want to believe.

Do what you want to do.

Feel how you want to feel.

I might steal a dollar, but I won't lie for one

I don't even have to know him to cry for son

My Gang letting off,

I didn't even know they brought their guns.

I pray for one of us to make it,

Just to bring the old times back

Table looking crazy celebrating a pack.

Loud Cognac splitting up stacks.

When the team gotta speak

Tell my lady to put music on

and vacuum the rug

when we catch our enemies

we going to put their ass in the tub

who want to fuck with the plug?
The outside crazy
but the inside different
it's more uncomfortable than
shitting in the club
go in your house and remove all the bulbs,
I'm a light it up when I want.
Take your car and remove all the lugs.
and tell you don't screw with me.
I was put in the position.
I ain't ask for it.
They just like the ethic.
Wait till the work is done.
Pour a glass for it.
My Gang running wild.
You can get it if you ask for it.
Drip cannon ball
Splash for it
Be careful what you ask for.
Cause they do it for it.

Sirens

Coup looks like a Decepticon

Doors go up that shit transform.

We get it on get it on

Hit the jackpot, money long.

Spin off until the tires are worn.

Between that and the purp

Its cloudier than a storm

Setting off all the alarms

We want all the smoke.

Spill all your yolk.

Not fucking with us, then that's all she wrote.

Silencers silence all that you know.

When my henchmen henceforth

You have to go.

Got a business to uphold.

Tonge numb off the blow.

Do as them so

Cement ankles toss them over boats.
They will never float.
Raw uncut I will never coat.
Take care of the news before they bloat.
The game is cold.
I'm not stabbing, I'm poking.
Not strapped just holding
Wont sleep or even rest
I don't protest, I protect.
Pumping like a piston
Can't roll what we are smoking.
Leave you coughing and choking.
We are eating come and get a taste.
I'm driven but I'm cruising.
Try to live the life that is meant to be lived.

When did sirens become like violins?
Stuck to the game like a siemens.
We about that, riding until we are dying.

The year karma came back

Sometimes an eye for an eye doesn't end there

It could be a fingers Lungs and your life of fear

There's God on one shoulder and the devil on the other, covers

The odds over the kettle burning being colder the bluffer, sufferer

Or

The job to holder in anything unsettled

King of ushers, lover

I walk to a ASU battle of percussions

Proud and noble back handing anyone with a discussion

Sometimes I feel punished

All the life or death

Did my best under stress

But I know it's not for nothing

Till my last breath is left

Sit behind a desk high still fresh

On becoming something

I just want to make my mama proud and shine from clouds

My head bowed knees on the ground

Overcharged destined electric

I am found place the crown

Only thing left is animal crowds and sounds

Drawn to me the Alpha Beast no defeat climbing peaks kinetic

Mindset to slaughter Goats can't rely on hope

When I don't know no one lowers ropes

Blink and see the beginning

A win is a win but I'm not finished

My antidote wasn't with sugars coats

You can quote this next note

The line has been the thinnest and spinning

Demons are waiting for me to lose my gripping and start slipping

But karma came back this year with new living
and billing

Incognito & Inconspicuous

I been watching the outside

East west north and the south side

Word this ain't going to nothing but getting mine

One way in one way out lined

Death or hard time

It's me and you no one has to know about our crime

You got tellers the custies and the guards all mine

Everybody get down and don't move and you won't die

Matter fact close your eyes

Disguise

A good reason to hide

As bikers we would do better on motorcycles

Put the machine gun rifle

All in their face and say open the safe

Pick up the pace

Stay positive I love the way it combinates

Fill both back packs

Now it's time to get away

No sounds of a siren

Calm your shakes

Swap out to a Corolla

Then to a station no more looking over your shoulder

Just another mile away it's over

I'm finally at my residence

Don't buy any expensive shit

Nothing you would draw attention with

Don't even seek penitence

Consider it Recreance

Remember what the objective is

Wait until it loses its relevance

Move through with caution in the messiest

You not the only one counting your presidents

Fuck I need a couple things

New jacket and some timberlands

New draws for my lady on my dingaling

Finance a Darango Gt

no name brand just black and white Ts

And hide the rest of the Benjamins

Broke ain't the only thing dead to them

But still doing what I do usually

No Lui V or jewelry

With more gas than a brewery

higher than your wildest dreams made by a greedy team

thieves hustle is reaching a duffel of green

I not judgmental

The need is monumental

Keep it simple

When climbing through windows

Only go for the essentials

Homes no rentals

Gold no silvers

In the streets so ungentle

Gun butt your dental

Own the Corner

Have to lock down the spiddot

Where they stop and get driddop

Turn the pizza shop to a restaurant

Beautiful ghetto woman that can cook

Good selections at a price that's affordable

Purple gold loyal as they come

Call it Royal Love

Then bought the barbershop slash hair salon

Music playlist like a club leaving realer than they was

Sign say A1

High end black wood floor

Gold ceiling glass chandelier above somewhere you can be proud of

Next over the connected corner store

Only selling healthy product for all us

Nobody out there selling drugs

Even the pigeons different, white doves

Organic stock goods

so clean you can leave your shoes

fresh fruit and vegetables

Named it long Live

So the liquor store was unacceptable

Made into wine with collectibles

Something responsible

That won't get the best of you

The Mansion Cellar

Turned the whole corner to something respectable and presentable

All this disparity designed to fuck up our clarity

Where the wrong choices become popularity

Addictive habits forcing charity

In neighborhoods where it's us primarily

Out those areas there's no similarity

Spanish Black Asians searching for equality and prosperity

I'm a rep until the death of me

It made me tougher but I can't help but think could there be a better me

Where outsiders fear to be

level of barbarity

I don't think anyone hear or see

Hustled on the corners I was blessed with longevity

Buy it back one day take care of the streets to show my sincerity

Detonate

Set the timer to the c4
Dark fire opening up the detour
Destruction allows you to see more
You can rebuild
But you can never have what you had
Before
The problem when you replicate
Is the person who invest in it
Ain't the same as the people who protected it
I'm one of one
Real as they come you can speculate
If tested under the same elements
You would Disintegrate
jump out and I never hesitate
One wrong move I will activate
Me and my niggas posted up grilling

Like a tailgate

When you sleep I stay awake

Times ticking this a bad time to

Take a break

Handle beef like we shaving steak

This clip heavier than thanksgiving dinner on a paper plate

Sounds like a 808

I say fuck you and make sure I punctuate

Middle finger if I want to abbreviate

I got a pamphlet on being great

You can't fabricate mind power if your body is out of shape

It don't relate

There's nothing new but there's many ways

NGU in what I do, one day king status as I lay eating grapes

Everyday like a mafia wedding

Drunk stumbling calls it insomnia legging

Wake up on an island to tilapia shredded

I have to live in that direction

I do what I say and pray for next level to manifest it

Anything against me count your blessings

I'm a ticking time bomb no doubt

with a haunting laugh and smile like the crescent

My evolution to what my success is

I'm a detonate soon as they get the message

Internally conflicted for eternity

Physicians are finished this is what

I'm left with

A predestined weapon

Embedded

Cerebral cortex

To the Cerebellum

Step in where hell and death is

With a cold beverage for leverage

My mind in question

Made in the USA
Columbia, SC
27 May 2024

a3f669de-af2f-4710-8e18-51f5362c8618R01